All About America

COLONISTS AND INDEPENDENCE

Sally Senzell Isaacs

KINGFISHER

NEW YORK

All About America: COLONISTS AND INDEPENDENCE

KINGFISHER
LONDON & NEW YORK

Published in the United States by Kingfisher,
175 Fifth Ave., New York, NY 10010
Kingfisher is an imprint of Macmillan Children's Books, London.
All rights reserved.

Distributed in the U.S. by Macmillan, 175 Fifth Ave.,
New York, NY 10010
Distributed in Canada by H.B. Fenn and Company Ltd.,
34 Nixon Road, Bolton, Ontario L7E 1W2

Library of Congress Cataloging-in-Publication data has been applied for.

ISBN paperback 978-0-7534-6513-4
ISBN reinforced library binding 978-0-7534-6581-3

Kingfisher books are available for special promotions and premiums. For details contact: Special Markets Department, Macmillan, 175 Fifth Ave., New York, NY 10010.

For more information, please visit www.kingfisherbooks.com

Printed in China
10 9 8 7 6 5 4 3 2 1
1TR/0311/WKT/UNTD/140MA

The All About America series was produced for Kingfisher by Bender Richardson White, Uxbridge, U.K.
Editor: Lionel Bender
Designer: Ben White
DTP: Neil Sutton
Production: Kim Richardson
Consultant: Richard Jensen, Research Professor of History, Culver Stockton College, Missouri

Sources of quotations and excerpts
Page 5, George Percy quote: *First Hand Accounts of Virginia, 1575–1705* from digital.lib.lehigh.edu/trial/justification/jamestown/time/num-01.02.18_exp-false_sc-593/
Page 13, Sargry Brown quote: www.pbs.org/wnet/slavery/experience/family/docs3.html
Page 20, John Parker quote: www.boston.com/news/local/articles/2007/04/12/if_they_mean_to_have_war_let_it_begin_here/
Page 22, George Washington quote: www.ushistory.org/valleyforge/washington/george2.html
Page 27, Benjamin Franklin quote: www.jmu.edu/madison/gpos225-madison2/adopt.htm
Page 27, William Pierce quote: www.usconstitution.net/constframe.html
Page 28, President's oath: memory.loc.gov/ammem/pihtml/pioaths.html

Acknowledgments
The publishers would like to thank the following illustrators for their contribution to this book: Mark Bergin, James Field, Nick Hewetson, John James, and Gerald Wood. Map: Neil Sutton. Book cover design: Michael Yuen.
Cover artwork: Shane Marsh (Linden Artists).
The publishers thank the following for supplying photos for this book: b = bottom, c = center, l = left, t = top, m = middle: Inside images: © The Art Archive: page 23t (The Art Archive/Gunshots) • © Breslich & Foss: pages 5tr; 6tl; 6tr; 8tl; 12t • © The Bridgeman Art Library: page 27m (Ken Welsh) • © Getty Images: Superstock pages 1, 25b; 9bl; 22 (The Palma Collection) • © istockphoto.com: (Duncan Walker) pages 1, 2–3, 30–31, 32; 4t (Stefan Klein); 14 (Steven Wynn); 17tr (Maher); 20tl and cover (Natalia Bratslavsky); 20–21t (Duncan Walker); 20–21 (Duncan Walker); 23m (Christian Carroll); 26tl (DNY59); 26–27 (Lee Pettet); 27t (Royce DeGrie) • © Library of Congress: page 24tl and cover (LC-USZC2-3186) • © TopFoto.co.uk: The Granger Collection/TopFoto pages 4tl; 7tl; 7tr; 9t; 9m; 9bl; 10–11, 11, 12b; 13m; 13b; 14b; 14–5t; 15m and cover, 16b; 18tl, 18–19, 19t, 20bl, 20br, 21t; 25t, 27tr, 28bl, 28br, 28tl, 29t; 4–5 (Topfoto); 18–19 (TopFoto); 25m (World History Archive/TopFoto).
Every effort has been made to trace the copyright holders of the images. The publishers apologize for any omissions.

CONTENTS

Introduction

Colonists and Independence looks at the most important part of U.S. history during the years 1600 to 1800. It starts with a look at the first Europeans to arrive and set up homes in North America. It explores how they lived, established settlements, and started to govern themselves. It then focuses on how the 13 British colonies were forced to seek independence from Great Britain and, having done so, formed the United States of America. The story is presented as a series of double-page articles, each one looking at a particular topic. It is illustrated with paintings, engravings, and photographs from the time, mixed with artists' impressions of everyday scenes and situations.

American Colonies
England's settlement at Jamestown

The story of the nation known as the United States of America began in the early 1600s. At the time, the country was a land of forests, mountains, rivers, and American Indian villages.

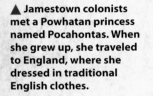

▲ Jamestown colonists met a Powhatan princess named Pocahontas. When she grew up, she traveled to England, where she dressed in traditional English clothes.

Meanwhile in Europe, 3,000 miles (4,800 km) away, kings, queens, and explorers talked about America. Did one of its rivers lead to a quicker route between Europe and Asia? Could there be gold hidden below its soil?

For the next 180 years, ships from England, France, Spain, and the Netherlands crossed the Atlantic Ocean. Their passengers came to America for a variety of reasons. Some were paid to explore and draw maps of the new land. Some hoped to find enough gold to buy themselves the best of everything. Some wanted to grow tobacco and other crops to sell back in Europe. Others came to get away from their busy cities and start a new life with houses and land of their own. The people who came to live in America were called colonists. They wanted to build a colony, which is like a small town. Leaders of such countries as England, France, and Spain built colonies in distant places across America.

▲ The European settlements of the early 1600s and the English colonies of the 1700s

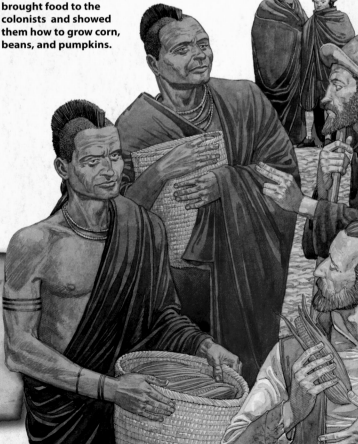

► The Powhatan brought food to the colonists and showed them how to grow corn, beans, and pumpkins.

Clues in the Dirt

We know about Jamestown from archaeologists, who dig up things that once belonged to the colonists and the Powhatan. These scientists have found beads, coins, bottles, weapons, jewelry, tools, and skeletons.

John White, a colonist, drew this picture in the late 1500s of Secoton, an American Indian village.

SECOTON

The Jamestown colony

A group of Englishmen arrived in Virginia in 1607. "There were never Englishmen left in a forreigne Countrey in such miserie as wee were in this new discovered Virginia," George Percy wrote when he arrived. Life was hard for these first colonists. They slept on the cold, hard ground. Many died from lack of food or from drinking filthy water from the swampy James River. Yet their colony survived to become the first permanent English colony. The colonists named it Jamestown in honor of England's king at the time, James I.

The colonists survived with help from the Powhatan Indian tribe, whose people had lived on this land for more than 10,000 years. Some Powhatan wanted to help the English. Others were taken prisoner and forced to show the colonists where to fish and farm.

▼ Tobacco leaves and clay pipes from the Jamestown site

▼ Houses, crops, and a church in the Jamestown colony

Settlements Before Jamestown
Around 1000 Vikings from northern Europe sailed to Vineland in Newfoundland, Canada
1564 France built Fort Caroline near Jacksonville, Florida
1565 Spain set up St. Augustine, Florida
1585 England tried to start a colony on Roanoke Island, North Carolina

The Exchange
The Powhatan taught the colonists how to farm, carve boats, and make clothes from animal skins. The colonists taught the American Indians about metal tools, brass pans, and guns. Another group of people came to Jamestown in 1619. Slave catchers captured black slaves in Africa, carried them aboard Dutch ships, and traded them to the English in exchange for food. Slaves were forced to work in the colony.

5

The First Pilgrims
Looking for religious freedom

In 1620, a ship called the *Mayflower* left the port of Plymouth, England, and headed toward Virginia. The wind blew it off course, and it landed in Massachusetts.

▼ Colonists used small rowboats to bring people and goods ashore.

▶ Pitcher, flask, and cups brought from England

Staying on the Ship

When they landed at Plymouth, the men took tools and supplies off the ship to start building houses. The women and children lived on the ship for six more months. Among the items they brought from England were the leather hat, leather water bottle, mugs, and containers seen here.

There were 102 English people on the *Mayflower*. Many of them were called Puritans or Separatists. They wanted to separate from some of the practices of the Church of England. Their beliefs were not welcome in England. The Puritans moved to the Netherlands for a while, but they became unhappy there, too, so they set out to live in the New World—America. These Puritans became known as Pilgrims. Besides the Pilgrims, the *Mayflower* passengers included a captain, a professional soldier, and some adventurers who wanted to make money in America.

An empty village

The *Mayflower*'s journey took 66 days. Most of the passengers got seasick on the stormy Atlantic Ocean. As winter began to set in, the ship finally landed on Cape Cod. They named the landing place New Plymouth. The Pilgrims found an ideal spot with cleared fields, fresh water, and tall trees. They soon learned that this was an empty village that the Wampanoag tribe had left behind. The Wampanoag had died from diseases carried by earlier European fishermen.

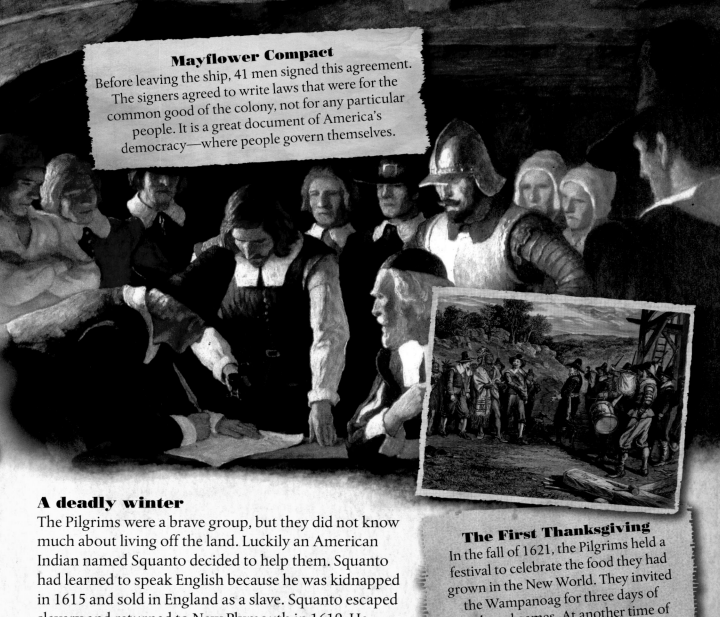

Mayflower Compact

Before leaving the ship, 41 men signed this agreement. The signers agreed to write laws that were for the common good of the colony, not for any particular people. It is a great document of America's democracy—where people govern themselves.

A deadly winter

The Pilgrims were a brave group, but they did not know much about living off the land. Luckily an American Indian named Squanto decided to help them. Squanto had learned to speak English because he was kidnapped in 1615 and sold in England as a slave. Squanto escaped slavery and returned to New Plymouth in 1619. He helped the Pilgrims talk to the local Indians and keep things peaceful. He also taught them how to plant corn, trap animals, and spear large fish.

The Pilgrims' first winter in America was deadly. They could not plant crops in the hard, winter soil, so they had little food. Diseases such as pneumonia killed half of the Pilgrims. The 50 remaining Pilgrims worked hard to stay warm and healthy. When spring came, they planted corn and picked wild berries. The next fall another ship, the *Fortune*, arrived in New Plymouth with 35 new colonists.

The First Thanksgiving

In the fall of 1621, the Pilgrims held a festival to celebrate the food they had grown in the New World. They invited the Wampanoag for three days of meals and games. At another time of year, the Pilgrims went to church on a holy day called Thanksgiving. In the mid-1800s, New Englanders combined the two celebrations into the popular Thanksgiving known today.

▶ The New Plymouth colonists celebrated their first harvest of crops. They invited Chief Massasoit. He brought five deer to roast over a fire and 90 Wampanoag guests.

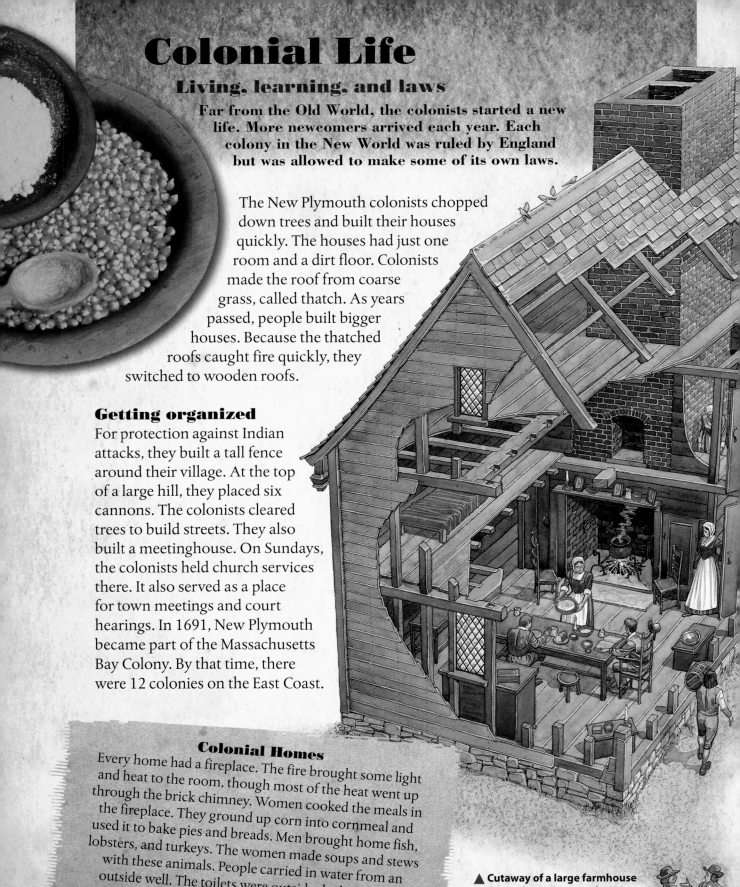

Colonial Life
Living, learning, and laws

Far from the Old World, the colonists started a new life. More newcomers arrived each year. Each colony in the New World was ruled by England but was allowed to make some of its own laws.

The New Plymouth colonists chopped down trees and built their houses quickly. The houses had just one room and a dirt floor. Colonists made the roof from coarse grass, called thatch. As years passed, people built bigger houses. Because the thatched roofs caught fire quickly, they switched to wooden roofs.

Getting organized

For protection against Indian attacks, they built a tall fence around their village. At the top of a large hill, they placed six cannons. The colonists cleared trees to build streets. They also built a meetinghouse. On Sundays, the colonists held church services there. It also served as a place for town meetings and court hearings. In 1691, New Plymouth became part of the Massachusetts Bay Colony. By that time, there were 12 colonies on the East Coast.

Colonial Homes

Every home had a fireplace. The fire brought some light and heat to the room, though most of the heat went up through the brick chimney. Women cooked the meals in the fireplace. They ground up corn into cornmeal and used it to bake pies and breads. Men brought home fish, lobsters, and turkeys. The women made soups and stews with these animals. People carried in water from an outside well. The toilets were outside the house, too.

▲ Cutaway of a large farmhouse in Massachusetts around 1670

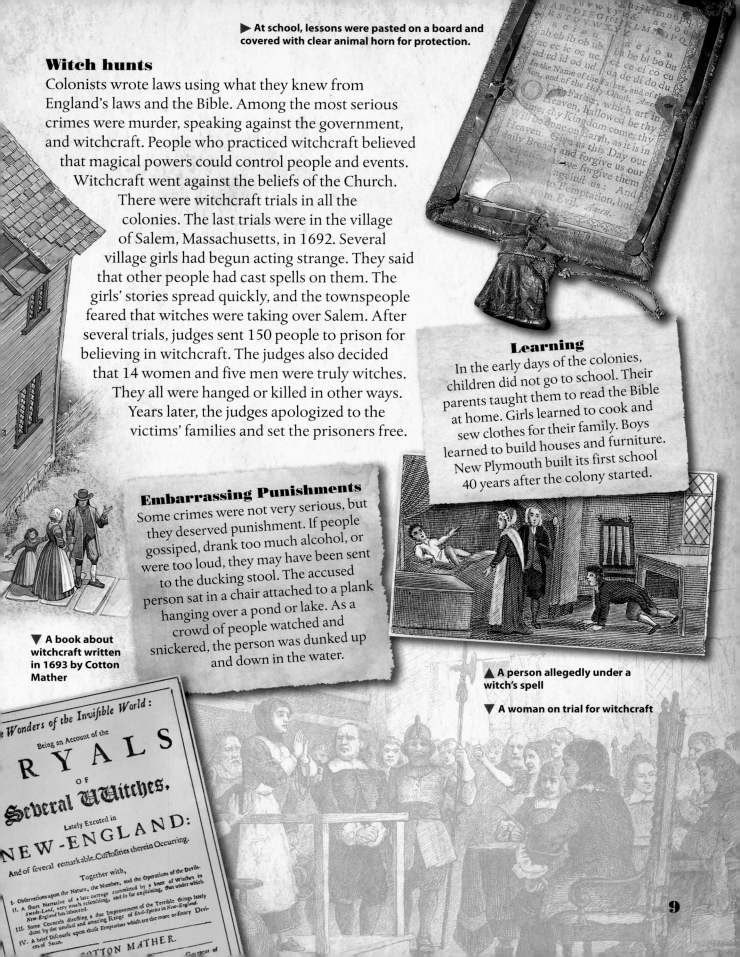

Witch hunts

Colonists wrote laws using what they knew from England's laws and the Bible. Among the most serious crimes were murder, speaking against the government, and witchcraft. People who practiced witchcraft believed that magical powers could control people and events. Witchcraft went against the beliefs of the Church. There were witchcraft trials in all the colonies. The last trials were in the village of Salem, Massachusetts, in 1692. Several village girls had begun acting strange. They said that other people had cast spells on them. The girls' stories spread quickly, and the townspeople feared that witches were taking over Salem. After several trials, judges sent 150 people to prison for believing in witchcraft. The judges also decided that 14 women and five men were truly witches. They all were hanged or killed in other ways. Years later, the judges apologized to the victims' families and set the prisoners free.

Learning

In the early days of the colonies, children did not go to school. Their parents taught them to read the Bible at home. Girls learned to cook and sew clothes for their family. Boys learned to build houses and furniture. New Plymouth built its first school 40 years after the colony started.

Embarrassing Punishments

Some crimes were not very serious, but they deserved punishment. If people gossiped, drank too much alcohol, or were too loud, they may have been sent to the ducking stool. The accused person sat in a chair attached to a plank hanging over a pond or lake. As a crowd of people watched and snickered, the person was dunked up and down in the water.

▼ A book about witchcraft written in 1693 by Cotton Mather

▲ A person allegedly under a witch's spell

▼ A woman on trial for witchcraft

Wonders of the Invisible World:
Being an Account of the
RYALS
OF
Several Witches,
Lately Executed in
NEW-ENGLAND:
And of several remarkable Curiosities therein Occurring.

Together with,

I. Observations upon the Nature, the Number, and the Operations of the Devils.
II. A short Narrative of a late outrage committed by a knot of Witches in Swede-Land, very much resembling, and so far explaining, that under which New-England has laboured.
III. Some Councels directing a due Improvement of the Terrible things lately done by the unusual and amazing Range of Evil-Spirits in New-England.
IV. A brief Discourse upon those Temptations which are the more ordinary Devices of Satan.

COTTON MATHER.
Governor of

The Colonies Grow

Getting down to business

By 1700, 12 colonies stretched from present-day Maine to South Carolina. New settlers came from England, Ireland, Scotland, Sweden, the Netherlands, Germany, and France.

Colonial villages grew into busy towns. Houses sprang up along the streets. Each family grew vegetables and herbs in a garden by their house. They also had a piece of land away from the houses where they could grow corn, beans, and other crops. Families also kept their cows out on these lands. Some colonists opened shops to sell goods. The blacksmith made horseshoes and iron tools. The cooper made wooden barrels and buckets. The wheelwright made wooden wheels for the horse-drawn wagons. Many colonies had fur-trading posts. American Indians trapped beavers, and then they traded the furs to the colonists in exchange for cloth or tools.

▼ **A typical colonial village**

American Indians Strike Back

The colonists were proud to own their houses and their land. The Indians did not understand land ownership. They believed that land belonged to everyone, just like the sky and the sun. As colonists took over more and more land, the Indians became angrier. Sometimes tribes attacked colonial towns. Sometimes colonists attacked Indian villages.

New Amsterdam

In 1624, Dutch people settled in New Amsterdam, which today is called New York City. In 1685, they built a main road and called it Wall Street. It became the center of business and banking.

▼ Ships pulled up to the New Amsterdam harbor to pick up and deliver food and goods. The colonists used goods from Europe for their homes and to trade with the American Indians.

◀ A label for tobacco that was sold in England

Other Exports

Great things grew in the colonies! The large forests provided enough lumber to send to England and to build ships to sell abroad. Tall pine trees made excellent ship masts. Fishing boats off the coast of Massachusetts brought in mounds of fish for the colonies and other countries.

▶ Pine tree shillings

Shipping out tobacco

Many Europeans headed for the colonies to get rich from tobacco. They had heard about the large farms, called plantations, in Virginia. The land was fertile and ideal for growing the tall tobacco plants. In 1640, Virginia shipped 670 tons (608 tonnes) of tobacco to England.

It took a lot of work to grow tobacco. A plantation owner, or planter, needed many workers to clear the land, plant seeds, collect the leaves, and press them into shipping barrels. Some of the workers were white indentured servants: The planters paid for their passage to America and gave them a place to live. In return, the servants worked for their masters for seven years. Many Virginia planters bought African slaves and made them work for no pay and with no hope of freedom. Ship captains sailed up the rivers to pick up tobacco and other crops at each plantation. Then they headed across the Atlantic Ocean to England. In return for these crops, the colonists received goods from England such as furniture, tools, and cloth.

◀ A water mill to grind flour or cut wood was often found in colonial villages.

Colonial Coins

The first colonists used coins from Europe, but they bought most things by trading. England did not allow the colonies to make their own coins. In 1652, Massachusetts decided to make silver coins anyway. One of the coins was called the pine tree shilling.

Slaves and Trade

Northern and southern colonies

In Virginia and other southern colonies, planters grew rich by selling tobacco, cotton, and rice. To get the workers they needed, they also traded in slaves, who tended the crops without pay.

Slaves had no choice about coming to America. One day they were living with their families in Africa. The next day, an enemy tribe sneaked into their homes, captured the entire family, and forced them to the shipping docks. Ship captains paid for the slaves with tobacco and other products brought from America or Europe. They packed the slaves into the bottom of ships as if they were bales of cotton. Slaves were carried west across the Atlantic Ocean in this way.

The heat, smells, and illnesses onboard slave ships were terrible. At least one-fourth of the captured slaves died on the journey to the colonies. In America, traders sold the slaves. Many slaves worked on large plantations in the South. Some worked in the fields. Others worked in the houses. They cooked, cleaned, and took care of the children.

▲ These leg irons kept slaves from running away.

▼ In this colonial store, craftspeople made tin items such as candle holders, lanterns, and pitchers.

Teens Learn a Skill
Parents paid craftspeople to take on their sons (and sometimes daughters) as apprentices. An apprentice worked every day with the craftsperson and learned how to make things. The craftspeople provided meals and a place to sleep. An apprenticeship lasted several years.

A Slave Auction
When they landed in America, ship captains took the slaves to an auction. People gathered at a public square to pick out the slaves they wanted to buy. The Africans had to stand on display. Their price depended on their age, size, strength, and skills. They were sold to the person who offered the highest price. Prices reached $1,000 ($30,000 today) per slave.

▼ Planters and businessmen at a slave auction

Making what they needed

Colonists in the North bought slaves, too. These slaves worked on farms or in their masters' businesses. Slaves cooked in the taverns and built ships in the shipyards. Slaves were sailors, barbers, and porters. England's lawmaking body, called Parliament, wanted England to earn money from the colonies. It wanted the colonists to send their lumber and goods to no other country but England. It also wanted the colonists to buy products that were made only in England. But in every colonial town, there were craftspeople who made goods for the colonists. Parliament was not happy to see the colonists open stores to sell their own things such as cloth and shoes.

▼ This painting from the late 1700s shows southern slaves having a few moments of fun by their small wooden cabins.

Charleſtown, July 24th, 1769.

TO BE SOLD,

On THURSDAY the third Day of AUGUST next,

A CARGO

OF

NINETY-FOUR

PRIME, HEALTHY

NEGROES,

CONSISTING OF

Thirty-nine MEN, Fifteen BOYS, Twenty-four WOMEN, and Sixteen GIRLS.

JUST ARRIVED,

In the Brigantine DEMBIA, Francis Bare, Maſter, from SIERRA-LEON, by

DAVID & JOHN DE

Slave Families

Slave traders tore families apart when they sold a husband to one planter and a wife to another. A slave named Sargry Brown wrote to her husband, begging him to find a way to bring them together. She wrote, "The trader has been here three times to look at me. I wish that you would try to see if you can get any one to buy me up there."

◀ An announcement of a South Carolina slave auction in 1769

13

Trouble with England

England's war leads to taxes

Before the mid-1700s, England's government did not get involved with the colonists' lives. That changed in the 1760s. England finished a war with France, which had cost a lot of money. It looked to the colonies to raise new money.

George III

In 1707, England and Wales joined with Scotland to become Great Britain. Thereafter, English people were usually called British. In 1760, Britain's new king, George III, thought of the colonists as his toys. He expected them to do what he wanted. If Britain needed money, then the colonists should pay more taxes. A tax is money that people pay to their government. The price of a tax is added to the price of goods such as glass, tea, and paper. A tax on paper made it more costly to print newspapers and to buy them. Each colony had a group of lawmakers, but Parliament did not ask them to vote on these new taxes.

▶ An embossed tax stamp made by the British government to use in America. The stamp was inked and then pressed onto paper to show five shillings of tax had been paid.

The Stamp Act of 1765

Britain made the colonists pay a tax on paper items such as newspapers, calendars, and playing cards. A stamp was put on each item to show that the tax was paid. The furious colonists tried to scare the tax collectors, who came from Britain.

▶ Colonist Ben Franklin printed a newspaper in Philadelphia in the 1730s.

Pennsylvania GAZETTE
THE

▲ Angry colonists

By 1750, there were more than 1,170,000 people living in the colonies.

No Say in Taxation

In Britain, subjects elected representatives to Parliament to speak for them on laws and taxes. Colonists were subjects of Britain, but they had no such representatives. They claimed they suffered "taxation without representation!"

French and Indian War

In Europe, they called the war between England and France the Seven Years' War. Americans called it the French and Indian War. Many American Indians helped the French soldiers fight the English. They thought it would save their land. Some Indians, however, helped the English for the same reason.

Fight for America

The king thought the taxes were justified. After all, the colonies were the reason Britain and France had been fighting. The conflict was over land. After the 1600s, many countries wanted a piece of North America. Spain claimed land in the west and Florida. France claimed the land by the Ohio and Mississippi rivers and in Canada. Britain's eastern colonies were growing. Meanwhile, the American Indians tried to continue their lives in all these places. Everyone wanted to spread out onto one another's land. France and Britain battled over the land in a series of wars. Although the wars started in the colonies in 1754, they spread to Europe in 1756 and lasted seven years.

A 1754 cartoon asking the colonies to work together to fight against France

The Treaty of Paris

Britain won the war in 1763. Then Britain and France signed a treaty that gave to Britain France's land both in Canada and to the west of the colonies as far as the Mississippi River, except New Orleans (which belonged to Spain). Spain, which had fought with the French, had to turn over Florida to Britain but still owned everything west of the Mississippi, called Louisiana.

British soldiers during the French and Indian War (1754–1763)

Busy in Boston

Sons and Daughters of Liberty

Until George III interfered, most colonists were happy to be British subjects. They worked, shopped, and took care of their families. Then came Britain's taxes, and people started talking about change!

At first, there were secret meetings. These started in Boston, Massachusetts, and spread to other colonies. Men gathered in living rooms to talk about the king's taxes. They called themselves the Sons of Liberty, and they came up with ideas to stop the taxes. Groups of women, called Daughters of Liberty, began to spin their own thread and make their own cloth. They made their own paper, too. They stopped buying anything made in Britain. It was not easy to decide to turn against Britain. Colonists argued with one another. Many still wanted to be good British subjects.

A Boston Home

A wealthy merchant's family may have lived in this house. Servants worked and ate in the kitchen on the ground floor. They slept upstairs on the top floor. The family ate in the fancy dining room on the floor above the kitchen. Next to the dining room was a parlor, or living room.

▼ A cartoon showing colonists' anger at the Stamp Act of 1765. Under pressure from the people, Britain removed the unpopular act in 1766.

▲ Big houses did not have front yards. They were built right next to the street.

An Emblem of the Effects of the STAMP
O! the fatal.

Send in the soldiers

King George III worried about all these meetings in the colonies. The Sons and Daughters of Liberty were hurting businesses in Britain with their homemade goods. They were attacking tax collectors, too. What would they do next? The king sent soldiers to Boston to keep an eye on these unruly subjects. The colonists hated to see the red-coated soldiers walking around their town. Before this time, people in one colony did not pay much attention to the other colonies. That was now changing. When it was time to protect their rights, colonists wanted to join together. In 1765, leaders in Massachusetts invited other colonies to send representatives to New York for a meeting. Nine colonies sent leaders to the meeting. It was called the Stamp Act Congress.

▲ Colonists in New York used this money to trade and pay taxes.

► Patrick Henry

Patrick Henry Speaks Out

Patrick Henry was a lawmaker in the Virginia government. His powerful speeches against Britain changed the minds of many people. In March 1775, he spoke to a meeting of the Virginia government that was held in St. John's Church in Richmond. He said, " . . . give me liberty, or give me death!"

Talk of independence

Several great speakers stepped forward to give their views on taxation. They included Samuel Adams and Patrick Henry. These leaders persuaded colonists to fight for their rights not to be taxed unfairly. By 1776, they would be talking about breaking away from Britain altogether. They talked about independence. The colonies did not need Britain anymore, they said. The colonists should rule themselves. These men took great risks: If the colonies did become free from Britain, these men would become great leaders. If Britain kept a grip on the colonies, these men would be punished!

◄ These colonial ladies still bought cloth that was made in Britain.

17

Rising Up
Boston Massacre and Boston Tea Party

The colonists hated the new taxes. They raged at the British tax collectors who spied on the store owners. They resented the soldiers who moved into their towns and set up their sleeping tents in the parks.

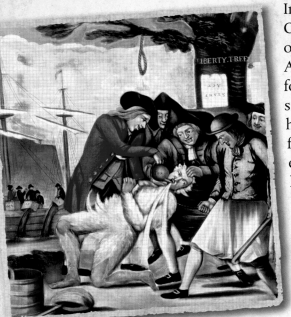

In Boston, bitter colonists often teased the British soldiers. On March 5, 1770, things got out of hand. It started when one young man shouted bullying remarks to a soldier. A crowd of colonists gathered quickly. Someone called for more soldiers. In minutes, the crowd was throwing snowballs at the soldiers. No one is quite sure what happened next. Someone heard the word "Fire!" Soldiers fired their guns and killed five colonists. This was a tragic event. Samuel Adams called it the Boston Massacre, and he made sure people in all the colonies knew what Britain's soldiers had done to the unarmed colonists.

◀ **Angry Boston colonists punish a British official. They have poured tar on him and covered him with feathers.**

▼ **The Boston Massacre**

What Really Happened?

Here's one explanation why the soldiers fired their guns at the Boston Massacre: The crowd of colonists dared the soldiers to fire their guns. One colonist teased, "Fire!" The leader of the British soldiers, Captain Preston, shouted, "Hold your fire!" The other soldiers heard only "Fire!" They thought their captain had told them to shoot.

Drown the tea!

More colonists turned against the king, his soldiers, and his taxes. On December 16, 1773, Samuel Adams led a group of angry colonists to Boston Harbor. They knew that a ship full of British tea sat there. If the tea were unloaded, it would be sold to the colonists, and the king would get his taxes. To stop this, Adams's men sneaked onto the ship and dumped the tea into the harbor. People called this action the Boston Tea Party. News of it spread to the other colonies. Colonists in New York and Maryland held similar "tea parties." King George III and Parliament were not amused. Parliament passed new laws to punish the colonists in Massachusetts. The colonists called them the Intolerable Acts.

The Intolerable Acts
Two of the laws that Parliament used to punish the Boston colonists:

1. Ships cannot enter or leave Boston Harbor. No goods will be delivered. No ships can leave to sell goods in other countries.
2. Colonists must allow British soldiers to sleep and eat in their houses if required.

▼ **Representatives at the Congress**

The First Continental Congress

As Britain punished the citizens of Boston, other colonies banded together to stand up for fair treatment. Twelve colonies (all but Georgia) sent representatives to the First Continental Congress in Philadelphia on September 5, 1774. These leaders decided that the colonists should stop buying British goods. They urged each colony to form an army to be ready to fight for their rights. They wrote a letter to King George and asked him to stop the Intolerable Acts and the taxes.

Continental Congress
The Founding Fathers of the United States came to the First Continental Congress. They included George Washington and John Adams. These men became the first two presidents of the nation.

◄ **An original letter about nonpayment of tax on tea**

Fight for Liberty
The road to independence

It was April 1775. In Boston, British soldiers were everywhere, dressed in their red coats. Nearby in the towns of Lexington and Concord, colonial soldiers prepared to fight for their rights.

The first colonial soldiers were just farmers and store owners. They collected cannonballs and gunpowder in a small building in Concord. British officers heard about the storehouse and sent soldiers to Concord to take the supplies. One colonist overheard the British plan. He ran to tell Paul Revere and William Dawes. These men, joined by Samuel Prescott, rode horses through the towns. They shouted warnings that the British were coming!

Minutemen grabbed their guns and hurried to the road near Lexington. Their captain, John Parker, told them: "Stand your ground; don't fire unless fired upon, but if they mean to have a war, let it begin here." Before long, the 70 minutemen faced hundreds of redcoats. Then a shot rang out, and more followed. Eight Americans died, and one British soldier was wounded. The British marched on to Concord. Along the way, minutemen fired at them from behind trees.

America's Symbols
Flag America's flags have long been red, white, and blue. One of the first flags had 13 stars for the 13 colonies, as shown above. Philadelphia upholsterer and seamstress Betsy Ross is credited with being the first to make this flag in June 1777.
Liberty Bell Made in London, England, the bell was hung above the Pennsylvania Statehouse in 1753. Colonists stood below it when they heard the first reading of the Declaration of Independence.

▲ The Battle at Bunker Hill on June 17, 1775

▶ Boston citizens saw copies of this paper, which listed those who died at Lexington and Concord.

The Bloodiest Battle
The Americans and British clashed again in June 1775 near Bunker Hill in Massachusetts. The British greatly outnumbered the minutemen. They fought the battle nearly face-to-face. More than 1,000 British soldiers and 400 Americans were killed or wounded.

A LIST of the Names of the PROVINCIALS who were Killed and Wounded in the late Engagement with His Majesty's Troops at Concord.

KILLED.
Of Lexington.
* Mr. Robert Monroe,
* Mr. Jonas Parker,
* Mr. Samuel Hadley,
* Mr. Jona. Harrington,
* Mr. Caleb Harrington,
* Mr. Ifaac Muzzy,
* Mr. John Brown,
Mr. John Raymond,
Mr. Nathaniel Wyman,
Mr. Jedediah Munroe.

Of Menotomy.
Mr. Jason Ruffel,
Mr. Jabez Wyman,
Mr. Jason Winship.

Of Sudbury.
Deacon Haynes,
Mr. ―― Reed.

Of Concord.
James Miles.

Of Bedford.

Of Danvers.
Mr. Henry Jacobs,
Mr. Samuel Cook,
Mr. Ebenezer Goldthwait,
Mr. George Southwick,
Mr. Benjamin Daland, ju, n.
Mr. Jotham Webb,
Mr. Perley Putnam.

Of Salem.
Mr. Benjamin Peirce.

WOUNDED.
Of Lexington.
Mr. John DeLoint,
Mr. John Tidd,
Mr. Solomon Peirce,
Mr. Thomas Winship,
Mr. Nathaniel Farmer,
Mr. Joseph Comee,
Mr. Ebenezer Munroe,
Mr. Francis Brown,
Prince Eaderbrooks,
(A Negro Man.

IN CONGRESS, JULY 4, 1776.
DECLARATION
BY THE REPRESENTATIVES
TED STATES OF AMERICA,
IN GENERAL CONGRE

◄ **The Declaration of Independence**

Famous Words

The Declaration of Independence said that people have the right to "life, liberty, and the pursuit of happiness." Britain's government was hurting the colonists with taxes, war, and punishments. So Americans would start a new government that provided "safety and happiness" for its people.

Declaring independence

During the fighting, the Second Continental Congress met. At first, it wrote letters to King George III and asked for a peaceful settlement. On July 2, 1776, the representatives voted to declare independence from Britain. The colonies wanted to be "free and independent states." Thomas Jefferson wrote the Declaration of Independence, and on July 4, 1776, representatives from each colony voted to accept it. A new nation, the United States of America, was born. It now had a war to win.

► **Colonial soldiers called themselves minutemen because they promised to be ready to fight in one minute. Mostly, they did as they claimed.**

Loyalty to the King

About 20 percent of the colonists were against independence. They were called Loyalists. About 7,000 of these colonists fought in the British army. Colonists who wanted to fight for independence were called Patriots.

◄ **Colonial minutemen had no uniforms. They fought in their work clothes.**

The Continental Army

Washington takes the lead

The British army was the strongest in the world. It was a huge, well-trained unit of fighters. The colonists pulled themselves together to fight for their cause. They started out as a group of volunteer farmers, but they became a powerful force.

The men in the Continental Congress tried to figure out how to win the war. The Patriots soon realized they needed one unified army. Each colony should send its soldiers, but they needed to be organized by a good general. Congress chose a representative from Virginia, George Washington, to be this leader. It was a big job to fill. A new Continental Army needed men, training, maps, uniforms, and guns.

On July 3, 1775, as Washington accepted the job, he told Congress: " . . . I beg it may be remembered by every gentleman in the room that . . . I do not think myself equal to the command I am honored with." Washington, however, was a good general. Through dark and foggy nights, he moved his troops across land and water to overcome the enemy.

▼ **The Continental Army wintered in Morristown, New Jersey.**

Dressed to Kill

When he fought in the French and Indian War, Washington's uniform had light-colored pants and a blue jacket. He wanted his Continental Army to wear the same. However, money and cloth were scarce, so many soldiers wore their own clothes.

A Wicked Winter

About 10,000 American soldiers spent the winter of 1777 at Valley Forge, Pennsylvania. Each day they waited for someone to bring them food, warm clothing, and shoes. Nothing arrived. Many soldiers died of starvation and disease that winter. Many others ran away from the army and went home.

▼ **Patriots defeated the British at Stony Point, New York, in 1779.**

▲ **George Washington at Valley Forge**

Washington's tired and injured troops were cared for by doctors, often outdoors.

▲ A rifle, pistol, and gunpowder holder from the late 1700s

America's soldiers

The new American government could not afford to pay for its army. This made its soldiers' lives hard. They could not live at home with their families. They slept in tents or cabins through freezing winters and steamy summers. Often the soldiers had no food, blankets, guns, or paychecks. Many of them stayed in the army because the government promised them free land after the war. Other soldiers stayed because they wanted to win independence from Britain.

The Revolutionary War

Britain and America fought dozens of battles from 1775 to 1781. Almost every colony saw bloodshed. Britain brought over its powerful navy ships to threaten the cities by the coast. In turn, America formed the country's first navy of 13 small vessels. In December 1776, Britain seemed sure about defeating the Patriots. However, one night, while redcoats camped out in Trenton, New Jersey, Washington sneaked his troops across the Delaware River. By morning, the Patriots had captured 900 prisoners. The British won some of the battles; the Americans won others. In 1778, France—Britain's enemy—helped turn the course of the war by sending soldiers and a navy to fight for the Patriots and America.

23

The End of the War

Victory for America in Virginia

For six and a half years, soldiers died of battle wounds, disease, and starvation. At points in the war, America's biggest cities fell into British hands. Still, the Continental Army kept fighting.

More than 25,000 American men lost their lives in the war. But all over the colonies, for every man who left home to fight, a woman took over his job. Women ran businesses and farms in addition to doing their own work. They sewed clothes and cooked for the soldiers. When deadly diseases spread through their towns, they nursed soldiers, as well as their children and themselves.

There were women on the battlefields, too. Mary Hays carried pitchers of water to her husband and other soldiers, who called her "Molly Pitcher." A famous painting shows her firing her husband's cannon after he was killed. Some women dressed in soldiers' uniforms. They fought and camped out with the men, who never knew they were women. Deborah Sampson and Anna Marie Lane were two of these secret soldiers. Both were wounded but survived the war.

▲ A famous painting of "Molly Pitcher" in action

▼ Americans shot cannons at the British at Yorktown, Virginia.

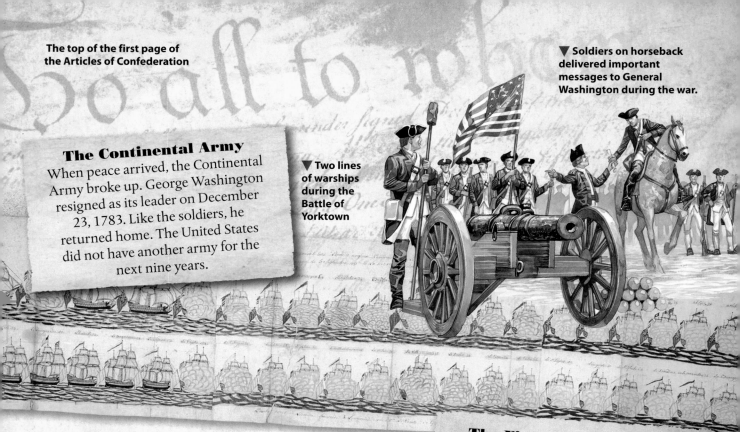

The top of the first page of the Articles of Confederation

▼ Soldiers on horseback delivered important messages to General Washington during the war.

▼ Two lines of warships during the Battle of Yorktown

The Continental Army

When peace arrived, the Continental Army broke up. George Washington resigned as its leader on December 23, 1783. Like the soldiers, he returned home. The United States did not have another army for the next nine years.

Victory at Yorktown

The last major battle of the war was fought in Yorktown, Virginia, in the fall of 1781. Britain sent 8,000 soldiers to Yorktown to try to take control of the South. By this time, Washington had the help of a French general, Rochambeau. French and American soldiers, plus a fleet of French warships, rushed to Yorktown and surrounded the British from land and sea. For nearly a month, blasts of cannons and guns filled the air. The French and Americans had the British trapped, with no way to get more supplies. Finally, on October 16, a British officer stood on a hill and waved a white handkerchief. This action was a well-known signal to stop fighting and start talking. On October 19, the British soldiers left Yorktown. The Americans marched them to prison camps. On September 3, 1783, American and British leaders signed a peace treaty in Paris, France. By November 1783, all British troops had left America. The new nation was now at peace with the world.

The First U.S. Government

In 1781, the states agreed to rules for their first national government. The document was called the Articles of Confederation. It loosely tied the states together as a nation. Americans were afraid to take too much power away from the states, so the national government could not make people pay taxes or send soldiers to war. The states sent representatives to Congress, but there was no president of the country.

▲ Britain's General Cornwallis surrendered at Yorktown on October 19, 1781. The American artist John Trumbull painted this picture.

A New Government

The states work together

In 1787, there were 13 states near the Atlantic Ocean. The question was: How could all Americans enjoy freedom and liberty and still have laws that tied them together as a nation?

In May 1787, the states sent representatives, called delegates, to Philadelphia to talk about a government plan for the United States. This meeting was called the Constitutional Convention. The states were very different from one another and cared about different problems. Most people in the southern states lived on big farms. In the northern states, more people lived in cities and seaports. Some states, such as Virginia, had many people. States such as New Jersey had fewer. Until this time, the states had acted like separate countries; they passed their own laws and printed their own money. At first, the delegates talked about the Articles of Confederation. They decided that this plan of government was weak. The states were not working as one, and this would keep the United States from becoming a strong nation.

▲ Delegates signed the Constitution with a quill pen and ink.

▶ The new government wanted a national dollar currency, not a variety of banknotes like these.

History Repeated

The Constitutional Convention was held in Independence Hall in Philadelphia. It was the same building as where the Declaration of Independence was signed. There were 55 delegates from 12 colonies. (Rhode Island did not attend.)

▲ Delegates arrived at Independence Hall on May 25, 1787.

Working It Out

The delegates argued about every part of the Constitution. Benjamin Franklin thought they might go home without a Constitution at all. He said, "I think it will astonish our enemies . . . that our States are on the point of separation, only to meet hereafter for the purpose of cutting one another's throats." Finally, on September 17, 1787, the delegates agreed. They finished writing the document and signed it. Now they needed the people in at least nine states to vote for it.

Creating the U.S. Constitution

The representatives decided to replace the Articles of Confederation with a new plan called the Constitution. This plan described how leaders would be chosen and laws made. It set out what powers the states would keep and what powers the national government would have. The Constitution said that representatives in Congress would make the laws.

▲ James Madison believed in a strong national government. Many of his ideas were included in the Constitution. He is sometimes called the Father of the Constitution.

Fairness for states

The rules for the nation did not come easily to the delegates at the Constitutional Convention. They debated many questions. For example, when it came to voting on laws, would each state get one vote? Large states, such as Virginia, said no. More people lived in Virginia, so it should get more votes. Smaller states, such as New Jersey, did not think this was fair. The large states might decide all laws in their own interest. After much arguing, they struck a compromise. There would be two "houses" of Congress. One house, called the Senate, would have two representatives from each state. The other house would be called the House of Representatives. Larger states would send more representatives there than smaller states.

Washington Comes Back

George Washington was invited to the Constitutional Convention. He did not want to go at first. He was not sure it would accomplish anything. Finally, he attended.

At the start of the meeting, the delegates elected him president of the convention. William Pierce, a delegate from Georgia, said about Washington: "Having conducted these states to independence and peace, he now appears to assist in framing a government to make the people happy."

The Nation Lives On

President, powers, and rights

Delaware was the first state to approve the Constitution on December 7, 1787. New Hampshire was the ninth on June 21, 1788. That day, the Constitution became the "law of the land." Its rules are just as important now.

U. S. citizens still follow the Constitution when they elect leaders and make laws. If people think that a law is unfair, they may ask judges to decide if it is "unconstitutional." That means it goes against what the Constitution says. The Constitution even has rules for making amendments, or changes, to it. It takes a long time to add an amendment. Both houses of Congress must pass it. Then three-fourths of the states must vote "yes" for it.

The Constitution separates government into three branches. The president is head of the executive branch. Congress is the legislative branch. Judges and courts make up the judicial branch. With these separate branches, no one person or group can be too powerful.

▲ George Washington knew he was an important leader. Still, he never wanted to be treated like a king. When some people wanted to call him Your Majesty, he insisted on Mr. President.

Head of the nation

In 1789, George Washington was elected the first president of the United States. Once more, he left his home in Virginia and rode on horseback to the nation's capital in New York City. He and his wife, Martha, lived in a large house in New York. Many servants and slaves helped them hold large parties.

▼ Washington's inauguration in New York City

▼ An 1810 painting that shows pride in the new nation.

The President's Inauguration

On April 30, 1789, there was a ceremony to make George Washington the president. It was called an inauguration. He stood on the balcony of Federal Hall in New York City. He said an oath to promise to "preserve, protect, and defend the Constitution of the United States." Every president since then has repeated this oath.

FIRST in WAR,
FIRST in PEACE,
FIRST in the HEARTS
OF HIS
COUNTRYMEN

The nation grows

When Washington became president, there were 11 states. When he left office in 1797, there were 16. To become a state, the citizens of the state had to agree to the Constitution. Many of them agreed only if some amendments were added to it. People wanted these amendments to protect the freedoms of individuals. James Madison wrote 19 amendments and presented them to Congress. Congress agreed to 12 of them. The states accepted 10 of them on December 15, 1791. They were called the Bill of Rights.

That was around 220 years ago. The Constitution now has 27 amendments. The nation has grown to 50 states. There have been many changes, yet the strength of the first colonial people and the desire for freedom and independence are still strong.

▼ On his way to his inauguration, Washington was greeted by the citizens and officials of New York City.

Bill of Rights: First 10 Amendments

1. Freedom of religion, speech, the press, to have meetings, and to demand change
2. Right to own guns
3. Citizens cannot be forced to house soldiers
4. Right not to have homes searched
5. People accused of crimes must be treated fairly
6. Right to a fair and speedy trial
7. Right to a jury trial
8. No cruel and unusual punishments
9. Citizens have other rights not listed in the Bill of Rights
10. Powers of the U.S. government are limited to those listed in the Constitution

The Nation's Capitals

First the nation's capital was New York City. Then it was Philadelphia. In 1791, President Washington chose the site for a permanent capital near his home. Virginia and Maryland gave land to build the capital city, named Washington, D.C.

Glossary

accused blamed for doing something wrong

amendment an addition or change to a document

American Revolution (1775–1783) war in which the North American colonies won independence from Great Britain; also called the Revolutionary War

apprentice a person who lives and works with a craftsperson to learn a job

Articles of Confederation an early plan for the United States national government

auction sale where a person buys an item by offering more money than others

capital the city where the government of a state or country is located

colonist a person who lives in a colony

colony a small, new town that is built in a new country by people from a different country

compromise an agreement in which both sides give up something and gain something

congress a group of representatives who discuss problems; the U.S. Congress is a branch of government that makes laws

constitution an official set of laws

convention a meeting

craftsperson someone who makes things for a living such as furniture or pottery

declaration announcement

delegate a representative; a person who speaks for many people at a meeting

French and Indian War (1754–1763) war fought in North America between Great Britain and France

government a group of people who run a country or state

Great Britain the country formed in 1707 by uniting England, Scotland, and Wales

inauguration ceremony to put someone in office such as the president

indentured servant someone who agreed to work for a certain length of time for a person who paid for transportation to a colony

independence being free to do what one wants

intolerable difficult to live with

liberty freedom

Loyalist a colonist who stayed on the side of Britain during the American Revolution

minuteman a colonial person who volunteered to fight against the British

Parliament the government body in Britain that makes laws

Patriot a colonist who was in favor of the American Revolution

plantation a large farm where cotton and tobacco are often grown

Puritan a person who believed that church services should be simple and based on the teachings of the Bible

representative a person chosen to speak or act for others

right something that the law says you can do or have

slave someone who is owned by another person and is made to work for that person

tax money people must pay to the government

treaty written agreement, usually between two nations

witchcraft belief that certain people have magical powers

Timeline

1607 England starts a colony in Jamestown, Virginia

1619 African slaves arrive in the colonies

1620 Pilgrims arrive from England on the *Mayflower*

1624 The Dutch settle in New Amsterdam (New York)

1692 Famous witch trials in Salem, Massachusetts

1707 England, Scotland, and Wales unite to form Great Britain

1754 The French and Indian War begins

1760 George III becomes the king of Great Britain

1763 The French and Indian War (linked to the Seven Years' War in Europe, 1756–1763) ends

1765 Britain's Stamp Act makes the colonists pay taxes on newspapers, legal documents, magazines, and other paper items; nine colonies send representatives to the Stamp Act Congress

1766 Britain ends the Stamp Act tax

1770 Five colonists are killed in the Boston Massacre

1773 The Boston Tea Party

1774 Parliament passes the Intolerable Acts; First Continental Congress meets in Philadelphia

1775 Battles of Lexington and Concord begin the American Revolution; the Battle at Bunker Hill; George Washington takes command of the Continental Army

1776 The Second Continental Congress agrees to the Declaration of Independence

1778 France joins the war to fight against Britain

1781 Americans win the Battle of Yorktown, and the British surrender the war; the Articles of Confederation become the nation's first constitution

1783 Britain and America sign a treaty in which Britain agrees that the colonies are free states

1787 The Constitutional Convention meets; the delegates agree on the Constitution; Delaware is the first state to approve the Constitution

1788 New Hampshire is the ninth state to approve

1789 George Washington becomes the first president of the United States of America

1791 The Bill of Rights is added to the Constitution

1797 John Adams becomes the second president

Information

WEBSITES

America's Story from America's Library (of Congress)
**www.americaslibrary.gov/jb/colonial/jb_
colonial_subj.html**

Ben's Guide to U.S. Government for Kids
http://bensguide.gpo.gov/3-5/index.html

Congress for Kids
**www.congressforkids.net/Independence_
index.htm**

Historic Jamestowne (National Park Service)
www.nps.gov/jame/historyculture/index.htm

Plimoth Plantation
www.plimoth.org/

The White House and President
www.whitehouse.gov/

Boston National Historical Park
www.nps.gov/bost/index.htm

BOOKS TO READ

Cook, Peter. *You Wouldn't Want to Sail on the Mayflower!* Danbury, CT: Franklin Watts, 2005.

Isaacs, Sally Senzell. *Understanding the U.S. Constitution.* New York: Crabtree Publishing Company, 2009.

Marsh, Carole. *The Mystery at Jamestown.* Atlanta: Gallopade International, 2006.

Peacock, Louise. *Crossing the Delaware: A History in Many Voices.* New York: Athenaeum Books for Young Readers, 2007.

Schanzer, Rosalyn. *George vs. George: The American Revolution as Seen from Both Sides.* Washington, D.C.: National Geographic, 2004.

Walker, Sally M. *Written in Bone: Buried Lives of Jamestown and Colonial Maryland.* Minneapolis and New York: Carolrhoda Books, 2009.

Index